LOOk Closer

Birds

06

LONDON, NEW YORK, MUNICH,
MELBOURNE, and DELHI

Text by Sue Malyan
Editor Penny Smith
Senior designer Janet Allis
Publishing manager Susan Leonard
Managing art editor Clare Shedden
Jacket design Simon Oon
Picture researcher Sarah Mills
Production Luca Bazzoli
DTP Designer Almudena Díaz

First American Edition, 2005

Published in the United States by
DK Publishing, Inc., 375 Hudson Street,
New York, New York 10014

05 06 07 08 09   10 9 8 7 6 5 4 3 2 1

A Cataloging-in-Publication record for this book
is available from the Library of Congress.

ISBN 0-7566-1433-3

Color reproduction by Colourscan, Singapore
Printed and bound in China by Hung Hing

Discover more at
www.dk.com

Contents

Look for us. We will show
you the size of every bird
in this book.

Laughing cry

On the edge of the woods, a sound like laughter rings out. It's a bright green woodpecker, and it is searching for food.

Swoosh!

Did you know...

... A woodpecker builds its nest in a tree. It digs out a nest hole using its strong beak.

I fly to a tree, then hop up the trunk, holding on with my claws.

I'm feeling a bit peckish.

I use my long, sticky tongue to catch insects. Sometimes I poke my tongue into ants' nests.

These red feathers show that I'm a male. Females have black feathers here.

Green woodpeckers are 12 in (31 cm) long and can live up to 15 years.

Night watcher

At night, a barn owl
watches and listens.
It is waiting for a mouse,
vole, or frog to kill and eat.

Barn owls grow
to 15 in (39 cm)
long. They can live
up to 21 years.

These white feathers
help direct sounds
into my ears.

I snatch my prey
in my sharp,
hooked talons.

I'm watching you!

Did you know...

... An owl eats its prey whole. Later, it coughs up the bones, feathers, or fur in a hard lump called a pellet.

Screeeech!

My body is tiny, but my fluffy feathers make me look big.

Shy bird

At the edge of a swamp, a purple gallinule is hiding. It will dive underwater if it is frightened.

A purple gallinule can be 8 in (20 cm) long.

My feathers are coated with oil so water runs off them easily.

When I spread out my toes, I can walk on floating leaves.

I find my food in the wet ground. I eat seeds, insects, and dead fish.

I have long legs so I can wade through water.

Did you know...

... A gallinule keeps in contact with its family by making quiet clicking noises.

Just hatched

A few hours after hatching, this fluffy partridge chick is up and running. Its striped coloring helps it hide in the undergrowth.

My soft, fluffy feathers are called down. They keep me nice and warm.

A red-legged partridge chick stands 3 in (8 cm) high. An adult grows to 14 in (34 cm).

I'll soon be growing my real feathers, and I'll be able to fly when I'm just 16 days old.

Where'd our mom go?

I use my long toes to scratch around in the soil, looking for food.

Did you know...

... A partridge nests in a hollow in the ground. Here she lays up to 25 eggs. That's more than any other bird.

On the beach

At the seashore, oystercatchers sit in shallow holes called scrapes. They are guarding their eggs.

Oystercatchers can grow to 18 in (45 cm) long.

Can you spot my eggs? They look just like pebbles.

15

Did you know...

... This bird uses its beak to open shells. It pries or smashes them open and eats the soft flesh inside.

I'll be sitting here for weeks.

I don't just eat oysters— I like crabs, shrimp, and worms, too!

Bird call

Screech! An eastern rosella spots danger and screeches to warn its friends. Later, it finds fruit and seeds. It calls other rosellas, inviting them to the feast.

flap! flap!

I'm a friendly bird and I live with my family. Other rosellas live with their mates.

Did you know...

... A rosella's beak never stops growing. It is worn into shape by cracking nuts and seeds.

I'm a male. My brightly colored feathers help me attract a female.

crack crack crunch!

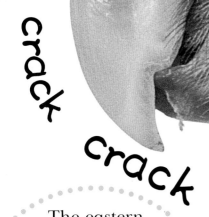

The eastern rosella can grow to 2 ft (60 cm) long.

First feathers

High up in an oak tree, a young tawny owl sits quietly. Its mottled feathers blend in with the branches and leaves, making it difficult to spot.

Tawny owls grow up to 15 in (39 cm).

I have soft, downy feathers because I am a young bird.

Did you know...

... An owl can look behind it by turning its head all the way around so it faces backward.

My feathers have fluffy edges that help me fly silently.

hoo-hooo

Feathers on my toes protect me from the bites of my prey.

Enormous bill

In the hot, wet rain forest, a Cuvier's toucan is having a snack. It uses its bill to break into a sweet passionfruit. Yum! Yum!

slurp slurp

My bill is nearly as big as my body, but it's very light because it's hollow.

A toucan's bill can be 5 in (12 cm) long.

When I eat, I lift up my bill and tip food down my throat.

Passionfruit is my favorite!

You recognize your friends by their faces, but I know mine by their colorful bills.

Grab a snack

From the edge of a stream, a gray wagtail darts out. It grabs a fly in its beak and holds on to the wriggling insect.

My tail helps me steer when I fly.

Did you know...

... When a wagtail perches, its tail bobs up and down. This is why it is called a wagtail.

I carry dirt from my nest and drop it in the stream.